Canadian Glossary
of
Fundraising Terms

John M. Bouza, CFRE

and

Doris M. Smith

© 1993

Cataloguing in Publication Data

Bouza, John M.
Smith, Doris M.
Canadian Glossary of Fundraising Terms

ISBN-0-9697767-0-5

Printed in Canada by M.O.M. Printing

Cover design by Paul Lafrenière

Mailing address:

John Bouza & Associates
202 - 16 Beechwood Avenue
Ottawa ON   K1L 8L9

Canadian Glossary

of

Fundraising Terms

To Canadian fundraisers
past, present and future.

Introduction

The field of fundraising is growing at an incredible rate in Canada. Less than twenty years ago there were 35,000 registered charities. Today Revenue Canada certifies more than 70,000 – a growth rate of more than seven new charities every business day!

Similarly, those of us who work and teach in the field find that nearly every day another new job has been created, another person has entered the profession, or another friend has decided to volunteer on a fundraising board or committee.

This is why we have recognized the need for this book. The *Canadian Glossary of Fundraising Terms* is designed to provide guidance and consistency among professional fundraisers and volunteers when discussing the work we do.

We hope the *Glossary* will become an indispensable tool for the dissemination of valuable knowledge as well as providing an explanation of simple terminologies. By its very nature, it should help board members, volunteers, and staff to do a better job of communicating their messages to the public, hence raising more money for their organizations and thereby being better able to fulfill their charitable missions.

Uniquely Canadian

Another important reason for writing this book is that Canadians must deal with the realities and distinctions of living close to the United States. This proximity permeates nearly every aspect of our lives and the field of fundraising is no exception. Many of the books, journals, educational sessions and professional associations that we as fundraisers read, attend and join are American. It is natural therefore that many of the terms used in fundraising originated there.

But, there are distinctions both in terminology and in techniques. To cite just one — while U.S. fundraisers frequently refer to mailing appeals monthly to existing donors, we know of no Canadian charity that is willing to be that aggressive.

Until now, the only reference for fundraising terminology has been an American publication produced by the National Society of Fund Raising Executives Institute. While it may be interesting for us to know what a *501(c)(3).* organization is, or that it must submit a *Form 990* annually to the Internal Revenue Service, it is totally irrelevant in a Canadian context. What Canadians need to know is that every registered charitable organization in Canada must complete an annual *T3010* form for Revenue Canada. But you won't find an explanation of this form in an American textbook.

And what of terms such as *census block groups* – something Americans use to describe sorting direct mail into small geographic areas? Canadians talk about an *NDG Presort* when we refer to the sorting that must be done to a direct mail piece in order to have it delivered to certain geographical areas by Canada Post on a discounted basis.

Furthermore, some terms that are used in U.S. fundraising have not become commonplace in Canada and do not appear in our *Glossary*. We have been involved with direct mail programs for over fifteen years and we have never heard the term *buckslip* (a slip of paper inserted in the mailing package that highlights the benefits of responding to the appeal, according to Mal Warwick, one of the most respected American direct mail consultants, in his book **Revolution in the Mailbox.**

Similarly, some terms from Great Britain occasionally enter our consciousness, such as *covenant,* even though it is not a donation technique available to Canadians.

Meanwhile, new fundraising terms are being created by professionals in Canada as they see unique circumstances arise.

For example, Ken Wyman, one of Toronto's best known independent fundraising consultants, has coined the terms *hooks and ladders* and *webbing* to indicate processes of actively uncovering networks of people you know, who can be useful in fundraising, on boards, as volunteers or as donors. And Stephen Thomas, Canada's leading non-profit direct mail expert, is popularizing the notion of *layering* in direct mail to indicate "a process of establishing a new direct response program on top of one already in existence". The example he uses is of the Red Cross having an established program to raise money for international relief and starting to raise funds for water safety in Canada, too.

American connection

On the other hand, many of the fundraising strategies and techniques used in the States are being borrowed and adapted for use in Canada. So it follows that most of the terms we use will be the same. In that sense, this book owes much to the inspiration drawn from glossaries and lists of terms found in a number of American publications.

About the definitions

This *Glossary* is focused on terms that have a special place in the field of fundraising in Canada. If a term is used but has the same common meaning as in any business or throughout the non-profit sector it is not included here. For example, the term "audited statement" is clearly important but since it is a common term whose definition can be found in any dictionary, it is not included in the *Glossary*. But if a term has a special "spin" that applies to this field we have included it. For example, an *audit* in fundraising terms is a specialized process of evaluating the existing fundraising strategy and techniques practiced by an organization, identifying strengths and weaknesses in the program, and recommending improvements.

We must also explain that, while we have tried to be as objective as possible with the definitions, there are certain issues about which we feel quite strongly and about which we have felt the need for a bit of editorial license in our comments. For example, while we recognize that cause-related marketing is a valid means of promoting a company and/or its products, and that charitable organizations often benefit greatly from this activity, everyone involved should be clear that this sort of sponsorship is not a philanthropic activity and corporations should not engage in cause-marketing at the expense of their community obligation to support charitable organizations with outright donations.

A First

Because this is the first effort at quantifying the terminology of the fundraising field in Canada and with the clear understanding that these are not terms one would simply translate, we have not made provisions for a French equivalent. This is a project best handled directly in French and perhaps could be done by a colleague who works regularly in the language.

Similarly, we're sure there are regional variations or terms which we have not been able to uncover. For instance, we know that casino nights are very popular in Alberta but we have not heard of any unique terms used for fundraising there.

This first edition contains over 400 entries. No doubt there will be omissions and other interpretations. If you have one, or know of a term that you feel should be included in the next edition, please send it in to us. If we use your term in the next book, you will receive a free copy of the next edition and your name will appear as a contributor.

Acknowledgments

The research for this book was funded with a grant from the **Voluntary Action Directorate, Department of Canadian Heritage.** We are grateful for their support of this project in its early stages.

We have benefited from the encouragement, support and active input from a nationwide network of friends and colleagues. In particular, we want to thank publicly the following who read all or parts of the manuscript and added significant editorial comments: Judi Angel, Tom Balke, Gordon H. Durnan, FAHP, D. Ray Pierce, CFRE. Stephen Thomas, and Ken Wyman, CFRE. We also want to extend a special thanks to our partner and Senior Associate Betsy Clarke, CAE, for her constant encouragement and much valued input.

Finally, we would like to thank our families for accepting and supporting our commitment to the charitable sector... with the long hours away from home that this implies.

John M. Bouza, CFRE

Doris M. Smith

JOHN M. BOUZA, BA, MA, CFRE has been involved in chari-
table fundraising for more than fifteen years. He is a *Certified
Fund Raising Executive* as recognized by the NSFRE. He is
President of his fundraising consulting company – John Bouza
& Associates, Consultants in Philanthropy. He has taught
courses in resource development for the Canadian Centre for
Philanthropy and Algonquin College, where he also sits on
the Advisory Committee of the Fundraising Certificate
program. He has lectured on fundraising for the Canadian
Centre for Philanthropy, Ottawa Fundraising Executives,
NSFRE international conference, and numerous individual
charitable organizations. He is Chair of the Ethics and
Professional Standards Committee of CSFRE. Clients of JB&A
range from small social service agencies to large national
museums.

DORIS M. SMITH, BA, MA has been involved in fundraising
and the non-profit sector for more than twenty years. She is
one of the first people in Ottawa to have completed the
Canadian Centre for Philanthropy Fundraising Management
Certificate Program. She has been a trainer with the
Volunteer Leadership Development Program and co-facilita-
tor of a (VLDP) workshop on "Developing Your Funding
Base". She spearheaded the drive for the Friends of the
National Gallery of Canada to raise funds for the reconstruc-
tion of the Rideau Chapel in the National Gallery. Doris is
presently a CESO Volunteer Adviser specializing in giving
fundraising workshops and seminars. She is an Associate of
JB&A.

John Bouza & Associates

Our Approach to Fundraising

Our philosophy is grounded in the belief that any resource development process carried out today, whether it be a capital campaign, an annual giving program, a special event or a sponsorship package must be based on certain key principles:

Fundraising is a process – It has a beginning, a middle. . .
. . . . . and no end.

People give when asked – For most people, the decision to donate to a particular organization is made in response to an "ask"; that is, giving is not generally spontaneous or premeditated. The purpose of the fundraising program is to give people an opportunity to contribute to your organization.

Ensure the mechanisms are in place – The way to give people the opportunity to support you is to build a fundraising program using all the techniques that suit your organization. You must put the mechanisms in place through which people will respond. If you build them, people will give.

An institution has no needs – An organization must consciously work to develop a sense that it is not trying to get something from the community (i.e., dollars) but rather is trying to give something to the community. Your institution does not need the money. Instead, you must stress that the community (local, regional and even national) needs the services and programs made possible by your organization. You are part of the solution, not the problem.

Partnerships – In the complex and often competitive environment of fundraising today, the recipe for success lies in creating a partnership among all the players involved. The successful project is one in which the vision is shared among the staff, board, volunteers, media, supporters and the community at large.

Market niches – No organization or campaign can be all things to all people. And no institution can expect everyone to support its campaign. With over 70,000 registered charities in Canada, and again as many non-profits, it is not reasonable to expect everyone to respond to every cause. The solution is to focus an institution's fundraising efforts on a clearly defined market niche and seek support from the segment of the population and those corporations with an interest in that niche.

Provide opportunities for giving – JB&A has a basic approach to fundraising that is exactly the opposite of the "starving baby" image. Do not cry out desperately for help, but rather offer people an opportunity to choose to become involved in a wonderful and worthy cause. We help potential contributors to see that it is in their best interests to help achieve the goal of the campaign. In short, we avoid "institutionalized begging".

Peer-to-peer solicitation – It is a truism, but none-the-less accurate, that people give to people. The most successful campaigns for large amounts of money are those in which people of means and influence are recruited to give their time and money to the campaign and to go out and ask others to do the same. Their task is to be up front, visible, and do the asking. All of this effort is backed by professional support and training as volunteers cannot be expected to do the background work.

A

AAFRC American Association of Fund-Raising Counsel, Inc. A professional association of major fundraising consulting firms in the United States.

ACAA Association of Canadian Alumni Administrators. (See CCAE)

ACFRE Advanced Certified Fund Raising Executive. A professional designation of the NSFRE indicating senior and highly professional status in the field.

AFRP BC Association of Fund Raising Professionals of B.C. (formerly F.D.A.). The local group for fundraising professionals in Vancouver and Victoria, British Columbia that brings together practitioners in that region for educational seminars and networking.

AHP Association for Healthcare Philanthropy (formerly National Association for Hospital Development). The professional association for health care institutions. This international association has an active Canadian chapter known as Region 13.

Accountability The principle that donation recipients must be able to inform the donor how the donation was used, as well as account for the fundraising costs incurred. (See Stewardship)

Acknowledgment A letter or note sent to thank the donor for the gift.

Acquisition Mailing A mailing to attract new donors or members. The same as prospect mailing. (See Prospect Mail, also Cold Mail)

Admail The trademarked term used by Canada Post for its targeted direct mail services.

Advancement A term used in university circles for the promotion of all phases of an institution's public activities including fundraising, alumni, media relations, high school liaison, government relations, etc. (See CCAE)

Advance Gifts Gifts made to a campaign prior to the public launch which serve to build momentum. Such gifts are usually solicited from supporters already close to the organization. Advance gifts are often crucial to the success of a campaign.

Advocacy Support of a particular ideology or cause; advocacy work may not qualify for charitable donation tax credit status.

Affirmative Statement The phrase that appears prominently on a reply coupon to encourage quick agreement to donate. Often begins "Yes, I will..."

Alumna/Alumnae/Alumnus/Alumni (Singular female/ Plural female/ Singular male/Plural male) People who have attended/graduated from an educational institution. Sometimes used for former clients of a social service agency.

Amounts, Suggested The gift amount that is being sought from a donor or prospect. Normally found on fundraising reply coupons to help the donor decide on the size of his donation.

Anniversary Giving (1) Donations made at a set date, usually commemorating a major holiday or significant event in the donor's or charity's history. (2) A method of encouraging donors to contribute on the anniversary of their last gift.

Annual Giving The term used to describe an on-going, regular fundraising program - as distinct from a capital campaign or planned giving.

Annuities, Charitable An irrevocable contribution of capital to a charity in exchange for immediate guaranteed payments to the individual for life at a specified rate depending on life expectancy. This is a common fundraising technique in the United States, but is limited in Canada because "while a charitable organization...may enter into such arrangements without jeopardizing its charitable status, a charitable foundation...may not do so." (Source: Revenue Canada)

Anonymous gift A gift which the donor requests not be publicly attributed to him/her.

Appeal, Annual A request for support on a regular, yearly basis (or throughout the year), often to cover operating costs.

Appeal, Special An extraordinary request for support to cover unexpected or extraordinary costs.

Arm's length Revenue Canada Taxation defines "at arm's length" as a tax concept used to describe the relationship between taxpayers. Generally, individuals who are related by blood, marriage or adoption are considered not to deal with each other at arm's length. Whether individuals who are not related to each other deal with each other at arm's length is a question of fact. The arm's length concept is of prime importance in determining whether a charity is designated as a Charitable Organization, a Public Foundation or a Private Foundation by Revenue Canada.

Ask, The The act of asking for a gift, either in person or in writing.

Associated Charity Two or more registered charities may apply to Revenue Canada to be designated as associated. If the Department approves such a designation, income that a charitable organization disburses to a registered charity that has been designated as associated with it will be considered a resource devoted to the charitable organization's own charitable activity.

Audit, Fundraising An objective evaluation of an existing fundraising program to assess strengths and weaknesses and propose improvements, often conducted by outside professional consultants. (Also Diagnostic Report)

Auction A popular special fundraising event, normally disposing of donated items or services.

Auction, Silent An auction during which bids are submitted in writing, either anonymously, or publicly with name and amount of bid listed, during a fixed period of time at an event.

Average Gift Gross donations revenue divided by the number of donors. A rough measure of effectiveness.

Awards Dinner A popular form of donor and volunteer recognition; frequently used as an occasion for fundraising.

BRE Business reply envelope, with pre-printed return address used for direct mail appeals. Frequently includes pre-paid postage.

BRE Permit Permit obtained from the post office to use BRE's when the postage is pre-paid. The permit number is shown on the top right-hand corner of the envelope.

Back-Up A duplicate copy of the donor records kept off-site in case of disaster.

BADs Negative or hostile replies in direct mail as well as undeliverable addresses.

Back End Service A company which will input your donor data on a variety of fundraising software packages and also generate donor thank-you letters.

Bang Tail An envelope with an extended flap which can be torn off and used as a self-contained reply device.

Bazaar Popular special event organized by churches and other charitable groups with a large local membership. Bazaars attract bargain hunters. Goods and services are usually donated by members of the organization.

Benchmarks Specific levels of contributions reached at various stages of a campaign or project by which the success or lack of same can be measured at pre-set intervals.

Benefactor Contributor, usually in monetary terms and usually the source of significant dollar amounts. Often a term used as one of the upper levels of donor categories in donor recognition programs.

Beneficiary A person or an organization that receives support from any source (usually monetary support or gifts-in-kind): a charity that is named as the one to whom the benefits of a life insurance policy will be paid or is named in a last will or testament.

Benefit Any special event in which all the proceeds above the actual expenses are to be designated as a contribution for a non-profit organization.

Benefits The special ways of showing recognition to members and donors who have contributed to a cause. Different levels of benefits are usually assigned to the several categories of members and donors. Benefits that give significant market value rewards to the donor affect the tax-credit status of the donation

Benefit, Cost (See Cost Benefit Analysis)

Benefit Show A special event organized to receive a monetary benefit from a performance (theatre, dance, musical, etc.) through the sale of a donated block of tickets or other means of sponsorship.

Bequest The gift of cash or property by will or testament.

Bingo A popular game of chance that is frequently used as a fundraiser where licensing rules require the participation of volunteers and sharing a certain percentage of profit with charities. Bingo is more popular in Canada - and especially in Ontario - than anywhere else in the world.

Block Captain Person in charge of a team of canvassers who cover a block of streets during a house-to-house canvas or campaign.

Block Funding A funding arrangement with a government agency whereby a well-established non-profit organization receives a large block of funding for a variety of projects. This funding relationship is more entrenched than either project or program funding and is reserved for agencies with long-standing track records.

Blown-in A reply coupon or card that is mechanically inserted (or blown into) a publication before mailing and is not bound, stapled or glued in place. Designed to fall out when the reader opens the publication.

Blue Book See Community Information Centre.

Board In this context usually refers to Board of Directors or Board of Trustees who are responsible for the governance of charitable and non-profit institutions.

Board Member Volunteer director who is elected, appointed or assigned to serve on the board of a charitable institution.

Bonding A precautionary insurance agreement (bond) for persons who handle significant amounts of cash.

Bossie Bingo A game of chance in which a field is marked in numbered squares and participants bet on which square a cow will deposit a cow pie.

Bounce Back An additional donation that comes from including a BRE in a thank-you letter (or in a package of goods sold). Not only produces extra income but also produces a closer relationship with donors who become frequent givers.

Bound-in A reply coupon or card that is stapled or stitched into the fold of a publication before mail-out.

Bowl-a-thon One of the many "thons" that are popular with charities, tailored to the preferences of target groups; participants usually obtain pledges from family and friends. In this case the participants go bowling for charity.

Brainstorming A meeting of a small group of people (4 - 7) to generate new ideas in a free and easy manner, so as not to impede the flow of ideas; it is only later that the accumulated ideas are evaluated and, if accepted, assigned priorities.

Break-open tickets. A game of chance in which the player pays for a ticket which has covered tabs and which is opened to reveal a combination of figures similar to those on slot machines and can provide for instant winners. (Also known as Nevada)

Brochure A promotional publication used to publicize the cause or organization; can also refer to a special brochure to be used during a major campaign to attract attention and to explain the needs that will be met with the help of funds raised during the campaign.

Budget, Campaign Budget projections showing the costs that are likely to be incurred during the life of a campaign.

Building Fund A capital campaign that is specifically targeted to pay for the construction and/or renovation of buildings belonging to the charity.

Bulk Mail Large quantities of letters mailed simultaneously that qualify for special postal rates. Bulk mail must correspond to the sizes and configurations accepted by Canada Post and must be sorted as regulated by the post office.

Bulk Rate Special postage rates for Bulk Mail.

Burnout What happens to volunteers, donors and staff who have been overburdened by excessive demands and unrealistic expectations made on them.

CAE Certified Association Executive. A professional designation awarded by the Canadian Society of Association Executives.

CAEDO Canadian Association of Education Development Officers. Formerly CAUDO (University). (See CCAE).

CAGP Canadian Association of Gift Planners. The professional association for development officers who specialize in planned giving.

CAHP Certified member of AHP. First level of accreditation.

CARD Canadian Advertising Rates and Data. A publication that lists all newspapers, journals, and magazines in Canada with the advertising rates and details such as circulation figures.

CASE Council for the Advancement and Support of Education. The professional development membership organization for university and college fundraisers in the United States.

CCAE Canadian Council for the Advancement of Education. The CCAE is comprised of three groups: CAEDO, ACAA and PACE. Its mandate is to facilitate interaction and coordination among the respective organizations in order to further the total advancement effort of higher education in Canada.

CDMA Canadian Direct Marketing Association. A national organization for businesses and non-profits that use direct mail. (People who do not wish to receive direct marketing promotions can have their names removed from mailing and telemarketing lists by using the CDMA's Mail Preference Service/Telephone Preference Service).

CFRE Certified Fund Raising Executive, a professional designation of the NSFRE.

CPRS Canadian Public Relations Society. A national organization for professionals in the field of public relations.

CSAE Canadian Society of Association Executives. A national professional organization whose mission is to provide the association community with the means to be more effective and contribute to a better society.

CSFRE Canadian Society of Fund Raising Executives. A professional development network for fundraisers in Canada.

Caging Service The process of opening donation envelopes, preparing bank deposits, updating donor lists and producing tax receipts. Available from commercial service bureaux for charities that don't have enough volunteers or staff (or equipment) to deal promptly with large numbers of donations that arrive in a short period of time during a direct mail campaign or special event. (See also Front End and Back End services).

Camera-ready Artwork and text (copy) completely ready for the printer with all crop and registration marks, and placement of images clearly indicated.

Campaign A special, organized effort to raise funds and generate support for a particular cause, organization or institution.

Campaign, Annual An annual effort made to raise funds or increase membership usually lasting a certain number of weeks; may have follow-up components.

Campaign Cabinet The group of people appointed to lead a capital campaign. They meet regularly, under the leadership of the Campaign Chairperson; usually each member leads a Campaign Division.

Campaign, Capital An intensive, time-limited appeal to raise funds for construction or renovation of buildings, or the purchase of equipment needed by the organization.

Campaign Chairman Also referred to as "Chairperson". This is the person who leads all volunteers working on the campaign and generally makes a major gift. The choice of a Campaign Chairman is crucial to the success of the campaign.

Campaign Division Any one of the numerous groupings that are created during a Capital Campaign to segment the target audiences by logical categories such as major gifts, corporations, employees, etc.

Campaign Director The person who manages the overall campaign – either a professional on staff or a paid consultant hired on contract to handle a specific campaign. Sometimes called Campaign Manager.

Campaign, Endowment (See Endowment Campaign)

Campaign Staff Usually paid staff who work under the management of the Campaign Director, concentrating on one particular aspect of the campaign.

Campaign Timetable The plan devised before the start of a campaign, determining the beginning and completion of the different activities that make up the campaign as a whole.

Canadian Centre for Philanthropy, The Acts as the authoritative voice for a strong charitable and voluntary sector through research, advocacy and education.

Canvass Direct solicitation, usually face-to-face, house-to-house.

Canvasser The person doing the canvass.

Case Statement A carefully prepared package of material describing the reasons for an organization's need for support during a special campaign, as well as the reasons for meriting this support. Case statements can be external – prepared for the general public and special prospects who will be canvassed, or internal – prepared to brief volunteer solicitors.

Cash Cash, cheques, money orders and credit card donations to a chosen organization.

Cash Flow Projection A plan showing the expected timing for incoming revenue. Especially necessary when obtaining significant pledges for future donations.

Casino A special event at which gambling is allowed, a favourite with some charities where legal, and when gambling is not frowned upon by the supporters of the charity.

Cause The organization or activity on whose behalf support is being sought. Support may involve cash gifts or volunteer activities.

Cause-related Marketing The process by which a company markets its products or services by offering to make a contribution to a designated charity each time a consumer participates in the marketing program. The term was coined by American Express to explain their marketing effort in support of the restoration of the Statue of Liberty – each time a cardmember used the credit card a donation was made by the company to the restoration fund.

Celebrities Any high profile people whose presence or participation during an event or an activity will act as an inducement to others to participate in and support the cause supported by the celebrity.

Ceremonies Organized by charities to recognize achievement, to attract media attention and to increase member and supporter involvement.

Certified Cultural Property If a gift comes under the Cultural Property Export and Import Act, the institution receiving the gift must apply with the donor or on the donor's behalf to the Canadian Cultural Property Export Review Board to have the property certified.

Cultural property may be paintings, sculptures, books, manuscripts or other objects, whether manufactured or natural. The objects need not be Canadian in origin.

The Review Board may rule that any object is of outstanding significance due to:
- its close association with Canadian history or national life;
- its aesthetic qualities;
- its value in the study of the arts and sciences, or
- its degree of national importance.

Chair/Chairman/Chairperson The person in charge of a committee. The variations are optional and designed to avoid the implication of sexism. Also used as title of the person in overall charge of a fundraising campaign.

Chairman, Honourary Usually a "celebrity" or high profile individual who lends his/her name to the organization to increase the organization's credibility in the community.

Challenge Gift A gift promised on the condition that matching gifts will be given by other donors; the challenge gift acts as an inducement for others to give.

Challenge Grant A grant conditional to the acquisition by the charity of matching funds; the challenge grant acts as an inducement for the charity to increase its fundraising efforts.

Charitable Contribution A donation in cash or in-kind to a charitable organization; if within the regulations of the Income Tax Act, it is eligible for an income tax credit.

Charitable Deduction The amount allowable for deduction under the Income Tax Act for a gift given to a registered charity. (See Tax Credit and Tax Deduction)

Charitable Donation A gift in cash or in-kind given to a registered charity.

Charitable Foundation (See Foundation, Charitable).

Charitable Gift Same as charitable donation.

Charitable Organization. Revenue Canada Taxation characterizes a Charitable Organization as an initiator of charitable activities, as opposed to an organization that funds the activities of others. Typically, it is controlled by an independent board of directors or officers and is responsible for administering a charitable program or series of programs, and arranges for the conduct of its affairs through its own paid or unpaid employees, agents or representatives. Over 90 per cent of registered charities are charitable organizations.

Charitable Registration Number Identification number given by Revenue Canada to each charity that meets the definition of a "charity" under the Income Tax Act.

Charitable Remainder Trust A "donation" to a charity wherein the donor retains a remainder interest in the property - that is, the right to use the property for life and the charity gets it upon the original owner's death; if a cash donation, the donor receives income from the principal.

Charitable Remainder Unitrust   Term used in United States for type of annuity, not applicable in Canada.

Charitable Status   A status accorded to an organization if it has been accepted by Revenue Canada as a registered charity.

Charity   A cause, an organization or institution active in philanthropic work.

Charity, Registered   A organization that meets the definition of "charity" under the Income Tax Act and that has been registered by Revenue Canada.   To be registered, an organization must promote one or more of the following: the relief of poverty, the advancement of religion, the advancement of education, or other purposes beneficial to the community as a whole in a way the law regards as charitable.   Registered charities are strictly regulated and must supply information about their activities annually to Revenue Canada.   A charity may lose its registration if it does not conform to the laws governing all registered charities.

Checklist, Special Events   Listing of all the tasks that need to be completed to organize a Special Event.

Cheshire label   A small rectangular mailing label made of thin paper and glued onto the mailing envelope or reply device in a direct mail package; usually also carries computer codes identifying the list and mailing details.   The list may be run with 3 or 4 names across the page - called three-up and four-up.

Chinese Auction   All bidders must put their money into the "pot" (with a minimum bid) until a secret, pre-determined amount or moment is reached, at which point the last bidder claims the prize.

Clean-up   Final phase of a campaign, designed to sweep up any outstanding prospects and unfinished business.

Client   (1) The person benefitting from the programs of a (social service) charity.   (2) The institution that has hired a fundraising professional (usually a consultant) to advise, assess and/or oversee the institution's fundraising activities.

Clustering   A term that refers to the joining together of small, like-minded charities to form a single umbrella organization.   This reduces operating costs, and makes operations more efficient.   (Example: Ontario Family Living Association).

Co-Chairman/Co-Chair   Two persons sharing the chairmanship of a campaign; usually done to lighten the burden of responsibility.

Code, Campaign   A brief alphanumeric series designed to identify each element of a campaign; especially different lists in a direct mail appeal.

Coin Boxes   A collection container placed by some charities in banks, shops and other public outlets to collect loose change; need to be regularly serviced.

Cold Mail   (See Acquisition Mailing)

Commission, Percentage   A fundraising practice by which a person is paid based on income received by the charity;   a practice frowned upon by the fundraising profession as unethical; to be discouraged and avoided.

Commitment   Promise of a gift or pledge by an individual or an institution to support a particular cause.   Also used to describe involvement by a person or institution in the activities of a cause.

Committee, Ad hoc   Committee set up for a particular purpose and for a limited time only, until its task has been completed.   (See Task Force)

Committee, Fundraising A standing or ad hoc committee responsible for setting fundraising policies, developing and implementing strategies and initiatives, and soliciting funds.

Committees Structured groups led by a chairman and often responsible to the board of the organization. Committees put into practice the policy decisions reached by a board; most charities rely heavily on the work of volunteer committees.

Community Foundation (See Foundation, Community).

Community Information Centre An organization that exists in many communities that helps people in need find out about groups that offer help. CICs often publish a directory (frequently called The Blue Book) which lists help-giving organizations. A good place to find addresses for service clubs.

Community Investment A term, becoming increasingly common in the corporate world, used to describe a company's charitable donations activities; implies a responsibility on the part of the company to invest funds for the betterment of the community in which it operates.

Community Service Sentencing Requiring people convicted of minor crimes to work a set number of hours for non-profit groups instead of paying a fine or going to jail. Often administered by the Elizabeth Fry Society, the John Howard Society or the Salvation Army.

Computer-generated Upgrade Matrix A method of putting a different suggested gift grouping on the reply device of a direct mail piece depending on the size of the donor's most recent (or largest) gift.

Computer Mailing A direct mail appeal letter "personalized" with the help of computer programming.

Computer Service Bureau A business offering computerization of direct mail appeal packages and/or list management.

Computerized Data Base Collection of information about a particular subject stored in a computer system.

Computerized Donor Base Donor records entered on a computerized data base, using a specialized software which allows for effective use of the information thus stored for fundraising and record-keeping.

Concentric Circles of Giving The basic fundraising principle which demonstrates that the most likely sources for support of any organization are those closest to it; and moving progressively out to clients/users, and then the general public. *[illustration]*

Concentric Circles of Fundraising

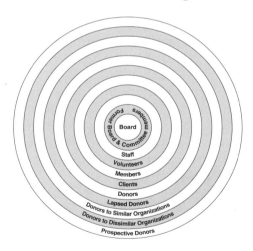

Conflict of Interest The principle which indicates that a person should not receive personal financial benefit from his or her involvement with a charitable organization or volunteer activity.

Constituency Those people with an interest in the organization, such as board, staff, volunteers, clients and donors.

Consultant (See Fundraising Consultant)

Contingency Fund Assets set aside by an organization for unpredictable situations or in the event that other funding does not materialize.

Continuation (See Roll Out)

Contribution Any voluntary gift of money, property, equipment or services to a non-profit or charity.

Control or Control Package A direct mail package that has performed successfully over time so as to become the standard against which new ideas or packages are tested and measured.

Copy Platform Written statement about the organization's mission, objectives and programs that is used as a guide for the preparation of all written material about the organization.

Corporate Donation A philanthropic gift given freely by a company to a charity without expectation of a benefit, other than a minor token.

Corporate Donations Committee A group of staff and/or board members of a company who decide on donations based on company donations policies.

Corporate Foundation (See Foundation, Corporate).

Corporate Sponsorship A method of corporate support for charities in which the company clearly expects a marketing or product sales return; not to be confused with corporate philanthropy or charitable donations.

Cost Benefit Analysis A method for calculating the financial costs and the revenues earned from a particular fundraising activity or technique; the concept suggests a concern for getting the most of something for the least cost.

Cost per Dollar Raised A term used in direct mail to analyze the value of the mailing based on how much it brings in.

Cost to Service a Member The total dollar value of benefits given to members, such as newsletter, booklets, and so on. The figure may exceed the dues charged.

Council, Advisory A committee usually composed of prominent community leaders, experts in the field of interest of the charity and "celebrities" who lend their names to an organization. Their advice may be sought on occasion and they may be asked to meet occasionally, but it may be their very presence on a masthead that is important. They help establish the credibility of the organization. (See also Council, Honourary)

Council, Honourary A group of prominent individuals who lend their name in support of a charitable cause. Often the members of the council are not required to participate actively in the affairs of the organization. (See also Council, Advisory)

Covenant British term.

Credit Card An option used increasingly by charities to facilitate payment of donations or pledges or monthly gifts.

Credit Cards, Affinity Major credit cards that are issued to supporters of a non-profit organization, usually bearing the logo of the organization, and for the use of which the agency receives a small benefit, generally a fraction of one percent.

Critical Path A planning tool which is used to schedule an event or activity. Beginning with the actual date of the activity, work back to determine the time needed for each component and the date by which each step must be accomplished.

Cultivation The process of involving potential supporters in getting to know an organization before soliciting a gift.

Cultural Property Export and Import Act (CPEIA) The Canadian Cultural Property Export Review Board (CCPERB) is responsible under the CPEIA for certifying that an object is of such "outstanding significance and national importance" that its loss to Canada would diminish the national heritage.

The Income Tax Act and the CPEIA provide tax incentives to people who want to sell or donate significant cultural property to Canadian institutions.

Cut-off Date In direct mail, the term for the date when the campaign can be considered to be completed. For analysis and planning purposes a consistent cut-off date must be used even though donations may come in over a longer period of time.

Deferred Giving (See Planned Giving)

Demographics The study and application of socio-economic characteristics and data such as age and income to understand donor profiles.

Designated Gift A donation for a specific purpose clearly stated by the donor. (See also Restricted Fund)

Development A term used to define the total process of fundraising; usually includes public affairs and marketing and takes a long-term approach to fundraising with a focus on the development of a relationship with donors.

Development Office The organized function within an organization charged with carrying out a development program.

Development Program The overall fundraising and public relations activities of a charitable organization; may include annual giving, capital campaigns, gift clubs, deferred giving, etc.

Diagnostic Report See Audit, Fundraising.

Direct Mail Solicitation of funds by mail; usually divided into in-house appeals to previous contributors and acquisition or prospect mail to potential donors.

Direct Response A broader term for Direct Mail that puts the emphasis on the reply rather than the appeal and may include telemarketing and other direct communication techniques.

Director of Development The individual who heads an organization's development program.

Disbursement Quota The amount a registered charity must spend each year on certain activities or to "qualified donees" to meet the requirements for continued registration. The quota differs for each category of registered charity. A Foundation (both public and private) must disburse 80% of receipted donations received in the immediate preceding year. This does not include bequests, inheritances, ten-year gifts and gifts from a registered charity.

Discretionary Funds Gift income that can be used by the organization's board and/or management as it wishes; that is, without conditions attached by the donor.

Dollars per Hour Measure of an event's effectiveness.

Donation A voluntary gift of money, goods or services to a charitable organization with no expectation of a tangible benefit to the donor.

Donor A person who makes a donation to a charitable organization.

Donor Acquisition The process of attracting first-time contributors to a charitable organization; often used in direct mail, may also apply to raffle tickets and special events.

Donor Cultivation The process of involving donors or prospective donors in the activities of the organization so that they will be more inclined to make a donation in the future.

Donor, Current A donor who has contributed recently to an organization; usually considered to be within the last eighteen months to two years.

Donor File The list of people, companies and organizations that support the charity, along with the details of their giving history.

Donor Identification The process of understanding the attributes and attitudes of a charity's donors and searching out similar prospects to become new donors.

Donor, Lapsed A donor who has not contributed recently; usually has not given in the last eighteen months or two years.

Donor Life Cycle The concept that an average donor will continue to contribute to an organization for a predictable period of time.

Donor List The overall list of people, companies and groups that support a charity; an extremely valuable asset of a charitable organization, to be treated as such.

Donor Profile (1) A file containing specific information about an individual supporter gathered through research. (2) A description of the demographic and psychographic attributes of a charity's supporters. Since different people support different causes, a charity must understand the profile of its supporters.

Donor Prospect A person, company or group that fits a profile of the charity's existing donors and therefore would be more likely to support the organization.

Donor Pyramid (See Pyramid, Donor)

Donor Recognition A program to thank and acknowledge donors based on the size of their contribution. Usually involves listings in public documents such as the annual report and plaques or certificates for the donor and for placement at the site of the charity.

Donor Relations A purpose-driven, focused part of public relations.

Donor Renewal Fundraising activities designed to elicit continuing support from donors.

Donor Research The process of understanding the interests and giving history and ability of a potential supporter so that the solicitation is made in the most effective manner possible.

Donor Retention The concept of working to keep donors actively supporting a charity. Just as in business, it costs much to more to attract a new donor (customer) than it does to keep an existing one.

Donor Upgrading A process of encouraging donors to increase the amount and/or frequency of their support.

Donor Wall A public display listing the contributors to an organization or campaign. Usually erected in a lobby or other common area.

Door Prize An item offered as a random prize to participants who attend a fundraising event. If the value of the prize is for more than a nominal amount, Revenue Canada does not allow the charity to offer a charitable donation receipt for any part of the admission ticket.

Door-to-Door Canvassing A fundraising technique involving a concerted drive in a short period of time going house to house soliciting funds. Traditionally done by volunteers, this is now sometimes being done with paid canvassers.

Doubling Day The day when half the total donations from a direct mail appeal have been received. This date is useful for planning purposes. Organizations find by experience that they have different doubling days.

Drive A campaign for funds usually with a fixed time element to it.

Drop Date The day scheduled for delivering a mailing to the post office.

Dues, Membership A set amount of money paid by a person to a charity. Membership dues are generally not considered a charitable donation, if the member receives tangible benefits in return, such as reduced or free admission to a museum or discounts on purchases.

Dup-elim Duplicate elimination; a term used in the direct mail industry for running a series of mailing lists through a computer program to check for and delete duplicate entries. (See also, merge-purge)

E

Ear-marked Gift See Designated Gift.

80–20 Rule The truism that twenty percent of an organization's donors will contribute eighty percent of the fundraising revenue.

Electronic Funds Transfer (See PAC, Pre-Authorized Chequing)

Employee Fund A source of donations inside medium to large companies that is collected from and distributed by workers, completely separate from the corporate donations budget. You find them by asking the personnel department or the CEO's secretary.

Endowment Principal or corpus maintained in a permanent fund the interest from which provides income for general or restricted use by an organization, institution or program.

Envelope, Carrier The envelope in which a direct mail appeal is sent; also known as an exterior or outside envelope.

Envelope, Window A carrier envelope that has a clear plastic panel through which the address of the recipient is visible.

Ethics A belief system which, in the case of fundraising, requires a high degree of honesty because of the nature of the activity; that is, handling the voluntary contribution of monies by donors to a worthy cause. May also include moral decisions not to seek or accept donations from certain donors, or resulting from certain methods, for instance, gambling.

Evaluation   A process of judging the effectiveness of any fundraising activity.

Evaluation should be the last step of a completed fundraising activity and the first step of any planned undertaking.

Every Member Canvas (EMC) or Every Member Visit (EMV)   A fundraising technique used frequently by churches, involving personal conversations and requests in the homes of each congregational member.

FAHP   Fellow Association for Healthcare Philanthropy. The highest designation for a professional fundraiser in the health-care field.

FSA   Forward Sortation Area. The first three characters in a postal code indicating a specific geographic area – a part of town in an urban area and the local post office in a rural area. Used in direct mail.

Face-to-Face (F2F)   Approaching top donors privately, not through the mail, phone or events.

Fair Market Value   The price a property would command in the open market between a willing buyer and a willing seller acting independently of each other, with each having full knowledge of the facts.   An official receipt for income tax credit can be issued by a charity for the Fair Market Value of property donated to it.

50/50 Draw   A type of raffle in which the winner keeps half the proceeds and the charity gets the other half.   Often conducted at a gathering of a group of supporters.

Feasibility Study A thorough and professionally conducted examination of the size and approachability of the market for a proposed fundraising drive (usually a capital campaign).

Fines Option See Community Service Sentencing.

Fiscal Period A taxation year of not more than 12 months' duration (or up to 53 weeks for a corporation). Such a fiscal period must remain constant unless the charity receives written approval from Revenue Canada Taxation to change the period before the change takes effect.

Flat List Address lists kept on letter-size pages instead of on index cards. The pages lie flat, not stored vertically like index cards.

Follow-up Mailing A mailing that is sent as a reminder to people who didn't respond to a previous appeal.

Foundation, Charitable Revenue Canada Taxation defines a Charitable Foundation as a corporation or trust set up and operated exclusively for charitable purposes which is not a Charitable Organization.

Foundation, Community A foundation that accepts donations and bequests from residents of a city or region which become part of endowment funds administered by the Foundation and distributed to worthy causes in that city or region. The oldest Canadian community foundation is the Winnipeg Foundation; the largest is the Vancouver Foundation.

Foundation, Corporate A charitable foundation established by a corporation to channel corporate profits in support of charitable activities. Has the advantage of being able to maintain donations in times when corporate profits are lower.

Foundation, Government A foundation established by a provincial government, generally with proceeds from government lottery revenue. For example, Trillium Foundation in Ontario and White Rose Foundation in Alberta.

Foundation, Parallel (See Foundation, Special Interest).

Foundation, Private According to Revenue Canada, a charitable organization or a charitable foundation. The characteristics that distinguish this category of charity from the other categories is the degree to which it is privately controlled or funded. In short, a Private Foundation is a registered charity that at the time of registration is controlled by a group of related persons, or receives over half of its funding from one person or group of related persons.

Foundation, Public A Public Foundation can be loosely described as a public body formed for the purpose of funding the charitable activities of other registered organizations. The most common examples of this category are "United Way" and "Donors' Choice" organizations. In addition, foundations created to fund the activities of a particular public hospital or school would normally be registered as a Public Foundation. While a Public Foundation is permitted to carry on its own charitable activities, most of its expenditures are made to "qualified donees".

Foundation, Special Interest A Public Foundation.

Freemium Front End Premium, that is, a free premium, i.e. a button, white ribbon, pencil, decal, or fridge magnet which is used to encourage prospective donors to respond to a direct mail campaign. (See Premiums).

Frequency The term used in direct mail to indicate how many times and how often a donor has given. Used to segment the donor list (See Segmentation, Recency).

Friend A term used by all kinds of organizations such as museums and libraries to indicate a group of active supporters – often both as donors and as volunteers.

Friend-Get-A-Friend Acquiring prospects by asking current donors to suggest people who might be interested.

Front End Service A company which operates post office boxes and will open and deposit your donor mail.

Fulfillment The act of completing a promised transaction, such as offering to send a calendar to all donors. An organization must assure itself that it has the capacity to "fulfill" the expectations it creates when it makes an offer.

Fulfillment Rate The percentage of donors who actually send in a contribution after having made a pledge to do so in response to a telethon, telemarketing, or other such effort to elicit their support.

Functional Budget Sub-dividing all expenses into specific projects and programs to show the true cost, including indirect expenses and an appropriate share of overhead.

Fund Raising/Fund-Raising/Fundraising The process of generating income for a charitable organization other than through the provision of its services. As a noun it is traditionally two words; as an adjective, hyphenated. Increasingly, as the field becomes more professional, the term is being used as a single combined word.

Fundraising Consultant An individual or firm that provides specialized knowledge and expertise in the development, implementation and/or evaluation of a fundraising program. A professional who works for a fixed fee, not on a commission basis.

Fundraising Costs Expenditures that are necessary to raise funds. It costs money to raise money. Acceptable percentages can range from 10 percent for a well-established cause to as high as 50 percent for a difficult cause. Start-up operations may not break even for the first year or two. Also some types of activities can cost ten cents on the dollar such as mail appeals to established donors while others such as special events tend to be closer to fifty cents spent per dollar raised. These percentages do not include volunteer labour.

Games of Chance Any of the techniques such as raffles, lotteries, Nevada, Bingo, etc. which some charities use to raise funds and in which the participants have the opportunity to win prizes and/or cash.

Gift A voluntary transfer of real or personal property from a donor, who must freely dispose of his or her property, to a donee, who receives the property given. The transaction may not result directly or indirectly in a right, privilege, material benefit or advantage to the donor or to a person designated by the donor.

Gift Array The series of check-off boxes on a donation reply form which donors can use to indicate the amount of their contribution. (See also, computer-generated upgrade matrix) *[illustration]*

Yes, I would like to donate:

❑ $25 ❑ $35 ❑ $50 ❑ $75 ❑ $100 ❑ Other_____

Gift Clubs A mechanism used to encourage donors to contribute larger amounts by offering increased benefits and/or recognition at each higher level.

Gifts, Honour Donations made in honour of someone.

Gift-in-kind Donation of property, goods or services instead of money. Charities can issue tax receipts for the fair market value of most gifts of goods, but not for services.

Gift, Matching (See Matching Gift)

Gifts, Major Any gift which is substantially larger than the average for a given organization. Usually a concerted effort should be made to secure these gifts because, in well-run organizations, eighty per cent of the donations come from twenty per cent of the supporters.

Gifts, Memorial Donations made in memory of a loved one or friend.

Gift Range Table A chart showing the size and number of gifts that are needed to achieve the goal in a capital campaign. The table focuses the efforts of the campaign leaders on securing the largest gifts first. *[illustration]*

Gift Range Table
($3 Million Goal)

No. of Gifts	No. of Prospects	Gift Level	Amount Raised	Cum. Total
1	3	$300,000	$300,000	$300,000
2	6	150,000	300,000	600,000
4	12	100,000	400,000	1,000,000
5	15	75,000	375,000	1,375,000
8	24	50,000	400,000	1,775,000
15	60	25,000	375,000	2,150,000
30	120	10,000	300,000	2,450,000
50	200	5,000	250,000	2,700,000
75	300	1,000	75,000	2,775,000
200	800	500	100,000	2,875,000
Many	Many	Small	125,000	3,000,000

Gift, Specified A gift from a registered charity to a charitable foundation when the charities involved choose to make the transfer without affecting the disbursement quota of either charity.

Government Foundation (See Foundation, Government)

Grant A gift made by a foundation, corporation or government, usually for a specific project of activity and after submitting a grant application or proposal.

Grant Application The form used by a charity when submitting a request for support to a foundation or government funding source. Some funders have applications; others require a Grant Proposal.

Grant Proposal The document used when submitting a request for support to a funding source that does not have its own application form. Grant Proposals usually follow a well-established format in which all the necessary information is presented in a concise yet comprehensive manner.

Grantor The organization making the grant. Grantors are increasingly becoming more pro-active in selecting the type of charities or issues they will support and in demanding accountability and evaluations after the grant has been used.

Grantsmanship The process of developing grant proposals, conducting research, submitting applications, and engaging in the necessary lobbying to ensure that a grant proposal is approved.

Healthpartners A workplace fundraising campaign carried out in federal government offices as a joint effort with the United Way campaign to benefit 16 major Canadian health charities.

Hooks & Ladders   The process of getting to know people you don't know but need to know for fundraising purposes including finding mutual interests and then climbing the ladder of developing a relationship rung by rung.

Householder   A mailing that is sent to all addresses in a particular geographic area without a personal name or address. If names are gathered from some sort of list such as a phone book or public directory, the mailing is an "addressed householder".

I

IDPAR   Institute of Donations and Public Affairs Research. A research centre of The Conference Board of Canada providing information and analysis in the field of community investment and related public affairs matters.

IMAGINE   A community relations program run Canada-wide under the auspices of The Canadian Centre for Philanthropy to encourage individuals and corporations to donate more money and/or time for the good of all.

Independent Sector   (See Third Sector)

Individualization   (See Personalized Mailing)

Information Circular   Information notices published by Revenue Canada to clarify rulings and laws

In-Kind Contribution   (See Gifts-In-Kind)

In Memoriam Gifts   Donations made to a charity in memory of a deceased friend or relative. Often In Memoriam cards are available at the funeral home or a mention is made in the obituary.

Inter Vivos Trust A planned giving product whereby a donor promises (or contracts) to give a sum of money to a charity. The donor receives tax credit for the donation before he/she dies. Similar to an irrevocable charitable trust.

Internal Audit (See Audit, Fundraising)

Interpretation Bulletin Numbered publications produced by Revenue Canada to guide Canadians in the interpretation of government laws and regulations.

Insurance, Special Event Any of various insurance options for special events that limit the liability of the charity if someone wins a major prize, such as hole-in-one insurance for a golf tournament, or weather insurance in case of rain or snow.

Jail and Bail A type of special event wherein local celebrities are "jailed" and then must be bailed out by donations from friends and colleagues.

Job Description A written summary of responsibilities related to the performance of a position; can be used both for employees and for volunteers and committees.

Junk Mail By definition, any *unwanted* direct mail. With proper targeting most donors do not mind receiving mail from their favourite charities, thus charities must focus their efforts so that fewer people receive mail they don't want.

Kill List or **Kill File** A list that is used in direct mail of names that should not receive a particular mailing. The most common use is to avoid a situation in which existing donors would receive a prospect solicitation mailing, or people who have complained, or the CDMA donor preference list. (Also List, Nix)

Ladder of Communications Effectiveness A commonly used diagram which emphasizes that in any activity direct face-to-face interaction is more effective than less personal techniques such as flyers. Useful to remember for fund-raisers. *[illustration]*

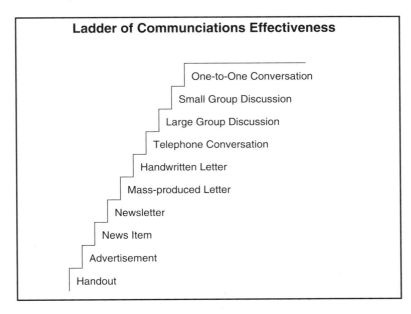

Ladder of Communciations Effectiveness

One-to-One Conversation

Small Group Discussion

Large Group Discussion

Telephone Conversation

Handwritten Letter

Mass-produced Letter

Newsletter

News Item

Advertisement

Handout

Lapsed Donor A donor who hasn't made a donation over the previous 12 or 18 months. Requires special renewal appeals. See LYBNT and WHYFU.

Layering The process of establishing a new direct response program on top of one already in existence; an agency that has an international program may add one for a domestic cause in which it is also involved.

LCP Presort Letter Carrier Presort. The smallest geographic area used by Canada Post. Mail sorted by the sender to this level qualifies for the largest postage discounts.

Letter, Piggy-Back 1) A fundraising letter that is included in a larger, unrelated package, such as a mailing from a union or church; 2) a letter sent as a follow-up to a previous letter.

Lettershop The company that is used to put together the mailing in direct mail fundraising. The collating, inserting, labeling, imprinting of postage, and sorting by postal code walk are all done here. (Also Mail House)

Life Insurance Gift A method of making a major, deferred gift to a charity by making it the owner and beneficiary of a life insurance policy. This may be done with either an existing or a new policy; and the premiums paid by the donor are considered charitable donations which are tax-creditable.

Lift Letter A secondary letter or note enclosed with a fundraising letter that is designed to add credibility, or additional giving incentives; perhaps signed by a celebrity or other high profile individual.

List The term used in direct mail to refer to the names and addresses of a particular group of people with a common characteristic, such as donors to a particular organization, subscribers to a certain magazine, people of a similar age in a particular postal code, etc.

List Broker An agent who arranges for the exchange or rental of the lists available from various magazines, compiled sources, or organizations willing to exchange their names. The broker acts as the go-between in the process.

List Cleaning Also, List Maintenance. The on-going process of keeping the names and addresses on a database up-to-date and correct.

List, Cold A mailing list of names that has no connection to the organization.

List Exchange The process of trading one organization's list with another's. The distinction here is that both agencies get to use the others' donor names and no money changes hands as it would with a list rental or trade.

List, House The list of people who are already donors to the organization.

List, Nix (See Kill List)

List, Rental The process of borrowing the names on a list for direct mail purposes and paying the List Owner a fee for the one-time use. The point is that the list is only "rented" for that single occasion; any future uses must be paid for again and the renter is not entitled to do anything else with the rented list.

List, Traded (See List, Exchange)

Loyalty Fundraising (See Relationship Fundraising)

LYBNT Last Year But Not This. A special appeal by mail or phone to past donors who have not given by year end.

Mail, Bulk Mail that is sent third class. It must meet minimum Canada Post quantity standards and be sorted and bundled in accordance with postal regulations.

Mail House (See Lettershop)

Major Gifts (See Gifts, Major)

Marketing, Direct Using techniques such as mail and telephone to reach directly to the customer/prospect, as opposed to broadly-based techniques such as advertising.

Mass Mailing A large-scale mailing campaign usually to prospective donors.

Matching Gift/Matching Funding The practice whereby a corporation, major donor, or government agency contributes additional funding (up to a specified ceiling) to match donations from the public. Can be used in direct mail, telemarketing, telethon, and major capital campaigns as an incentive to encourage donors to give to a special campaign. Matching funding is often discussed in terms of a 1-to-1, 2-to-1 or 3-to-1 match.

Membership A fundraising method in which supporters are given specific, tangible benefits and responsibilities in return for their contribution. If the benefits are substantial, the fees may not qualify as a charitable donation.

Memorials Donations made commemorating someone. It could be the donor or a friend or loved one, either living or dead. Organizations may establish a memorial fund and seek contributions from the relatives and friends of the person being memorialized.

Merge-purge A term used in the direct mail industry to indicate a computer program that merges a number of separate lists together then creates one master list after eliminating duplicate entries. (See also, dup-elim)

Mission Statement A brief description of the basic principles underlying the purpose of the organization; it's reason for being.

Monte Carlo Night (See Casino)

NDG Presort National Distribution Guide. The sorting, bundling and labeling by the first three digits of the postal code that must be done to a direct mail piece in order to have it delivered to certain geographical areas by Canada Post on a discounted basis. (See also LCP Presort)

Nevada (See Break-open Tickets)

Nix List (See Kill List)

No Show Dinner A fundraising event in which all the normal steps in creating a gala dinner are undertaken and tickets are sold as usual, only the participants are told they can stay home, there is no dinner, and therefore the entire amount of the event is a tax-creditable donation.

Non-profit or Not-for-profit An organization that is incorporated without share capital and which operates for social as opposed to commercial benefit. Registered charities are non-profits but there are many non-profits that are not charities, such as professional associations and sports groups. Only charities can issue tax-creditable donations receipts.

NSFRE National Society of Fund Raising Executives. The largest professional association for the field of fundraising in North America with a membership of over 15,000. The NSFRE provides educational support for the profession and has a two tier certification process in which it recognizes Certified Fund Raising Executives and Advanced Certified Fund Raising Executives. In Ontario there is a Greater Toronto Chapter of the NSFRE, a Vancouver chapter is also being established.

Official Receipt (See Receipt, Official)

On-Site Analysis A copyrighted technique for conducting an organizational audit for fundraising and other organizational development purposes.

"Other" The option which appears on the gift array of a reply device after the specific dollar amounts of suggested donations are shown.

OFE Ottawa Fundraising Executives. As association of professional fundraisers who participate in educational sessions and networking together.

OFN Ottawa Fundraisers Network. A grass-roots association of staff and volunteers working in fundraising who share information at regular educational sessions.

Once-A-Year Donors who say they don't want multiple appeals year round.

Outsert A printed leaflet which is included over the regular cover of a periodical.

• • • • • • *P*

PAC See Pre-authorized chequing. (Also Electronic Fund Transfer)

PACE Public Affairs Council for Education. (See CCAE)

P.S.A. Public Service Announcement. An ad placed free of charge on radio or television or in print media promoting a charity or its event.

Package, The The entire mailing piece in a direct mail program. Usually consists of an outside envelope, reply device, return envelope, appeal letter and sometimes a brochure, lift note or premium.

Paraskate A special fundraising skating/trade show event for teams and individuals designed to raise support for spinal cord disabled persons.

Parlour Meeting A small special event designed to encourage giving from mid-level donors (that is, people who give more than the computerized letter level but less than the personal visit level).

Pay Roll Deduction Plan A method of contributing to a charity by having a regular amount routinely withdrawn from a paycheque and automatically credited to the charity. Used by United Way and Healthpartners.

Personalized Mailing A fundraising letter that has the recipient's name, address and salutation on it; usually generated by computer. The name may also be laser printed on the outside envelope and reply device.

Philanthropy The philosophy and practice of giving voluntary financial and other contributions to charitable organizations. The word literally means "love of mankind".

Planned Giving A substantial gift usually made with estate and financial considerations in mind. The most common are bequests, life insurance and charitable annuities which often only take effect upon the giver's death.

Plaque, Donor A listing of supporters to a particular cause or campaign. Often with segments showing different levels of support in different sizes and placed in a prominent public location as a means of recognizing the support of the donors and encouraging others to join in supporting the organization. Also known as Donor Wall. Could also be a small plaque on one item or in one location.

Pledge A promise to make a donation at some time in the future. In the case of telethons, pledges are usually paid immediately after the event, and in capital campaigns, when the amounts are generally much larger, the pledges are paid over a period of several years.

Pledge Card A pre-printed form used by solicitors to obtain pledges from prospects in a campaign.

Pledge Flow Projection A report showing the amount of funds that are due to come in to a charity in the future based on pledge commitments made and the time when the income is due.

Pre-Authorized Chequing A method of making donations in which the donor signs a form and then a set amount of money is automatically deducted from the donor's bank account and credited to the charity's account on a regular basis; usually monthly. (See PAC, and Electronic Funds Transfer)

Premiums A product offered to prospective supporters usually as part of a direct mail package as an incentive to respond. A Front End premium is sent with the mailing (for example, the address labels of War Amps) while a Back End premium is given after a donation is received and may require a minimum dollar amount.

Product Sales A fundraising technique in which volunteers sell items in order to generate income. These may be unrelated to the mission of the charity, such as chocolate bars or raisins, or in some way connected, such as T-shirts with the organization's logo.

Prospect A person, company or group considered to be likely to give financial support to the organization based on carefully selected factors.

Prospect Mail A mailing to people who have never before given to the organization to attract them as prospective donors. (Also Acquisition Mail, ColdMail)

Pyramid, Donor The graphic representation of the segmentation of donors by type and size of gift with an emphasis on the need to understand the differing techniques required in communicating with donors at each level. *[illustration]*

Fundraising Pyramid

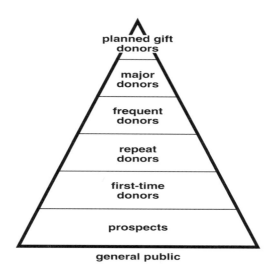

planned gift donors

major donors

frequent donors

repeat donors

first-time donors

prospects

general public

Qualified Donee An entity to which a Canadian taxpayer, corporation or charitable foundation may make a tax-creditable donation. Qualified donees include:

- other registered charities,
- registered Canadian amateur athletic associations,
- certain corporations providing low-cost accommodation for the elderly,
- Canadian municipalities,
- the United Nations or its agencies,
- certain prescribed universities outside Canada, and
- Her Majesty in right of Canada or a province.

Raffle A form of fundraising in which people are offered prizes in return for purchasing a ticket. Raffles are licensed and regulated by provincial statutes. Ticket price, whether large or small, is not eligible for a receipt for tax credit.

Recency The term used in direct mail to indicate the most recent date of a donor's contribution and used to segment the donor list. (See Segmentation)

Receipt, Official A form used to acknowledge donations of cash and gifts-in-kind. In order to be used for income tax purposes the receipt must conform to specific guidelines established by Revenue Canada. The donor needs such a receipt to support a claim for a tax credit or deduction for charitable donations.

Recognition, Donor (See Donor Recognition).

Records, Donor The system used to track all the essential information about contributors to an organization. Considered to be one of the most valuable assets of a charity. (Also Donor File)

Registered Canadian Amateur Athletic Association An amateur sports group that operates on a national basis, that does not qualify for charitable status but may issue official donation tax receipts.

Registered Charity (See Charity, Registered)

Relationship Fundraising The newest term for the preferred method of fundraising in the 1990s. The term suggests a structured program to develop and cultivate the on-going relationship between the donor and the charity. The emphasis is more on the contact with the donor than simply on the donations revenue. Sometimes very real, tangible benefits are offered to the donor, in order to strengthen the relationship. (See Loyalty Fundraising).

Remainder Interest (See Residual Interest)

Reminder Appeal Any mailing or contact with the donor that is done with the objective of urging the donor to respond to a previous appeal or pledge.

Reply Device or Reply Coupon or Card or Response Device The pre-printed form on which the donor indicates the amount of the donation to be made. It usually has a gift array and the donor's name and address already on it and often restates the appeal. Experienced fundraisers consider this one of the most important parts of the mailing. (Care should be taken to ensure that the reply device will fit inside the return envelope.)

Reply Envelope The envelope which is usually enclosed in a fundraising mailing for the donor to use to return the contribution. It has the address of the organization pre-printed on it and may or may not have postage pre-paid. Often a #9 business envelope. (If it has postage paid, see BRE)

Residual Interest A term applying to the situations where the owner of real property, after donating it to a charity, retains the right to use it for life, and the charity gets it upon the original owner's death.

Response Coupon or **Memo** (See Reply Device)

Response Rate The rate at which those receiving a mailing respond. Usually expressed in percentage terms. (Based on number of donations divided by number of requests sent out, less the Bads or undeliverables).

Return per Piece The amount of revenue generated by a mailing divided by the number of pieces mailed. Expressed as a dollar figure.

Revenue Canada Taxation, Charities Division The federal government agency that among its multitude of responsibilities is charged with registering and monitoring Canada's 70,000 charitable organizations.

Roll Out A mailing to the rest of a particular list after it worked successfully in a test mailing. (Also known as a "continuation")

Rummage Sale A fundraising technique used mostly by smaller charities in which mostly used items are gathered together, usually donated by supporters and offered for sale with the proceeds going to the charity.

Rule of Thirds A commonly used formula for capital campaigns: the top ten donors account for about one third of the campaign goal; the next one hundred donors provide the next third; and all the other donors contribute the final third. While there can be some variation in the amounts received in the top two thirds, the bottom third can never make up the difference for a short-fall from the top 110 gifts.

S

Segmentation The practice, in direct mail fundraising, of sorting donors into different categories based on the recency, frequency and size of their donations. *[illustration]*

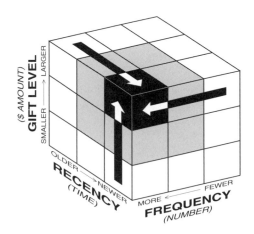

Sequential Giving A key principle in capital campaign fundraising that stresses that the largest gifts must be secured at the beginning of a campaign; followed by the next larger gifts and then on down the gift range table.

Service Club A group of people who help others by raising and donating money and/or labour.

Shinerama A fundraising activity for cystic fibrosis in which volunteers travel by foot through high density areas asking people if they would like their shoes shined for a charity.

Short Fat Guys One Mile Downhill Run A special event that originated in Halifax, Nova Scotia in which participants do as the name suggests. There is a hot-dog stand half way through the run in case participants get hungry. The beneficiary charity changes each year. As this is a trademarked event, other communities wishing to use this theme must pay a licensing fee to the creators.

Solicitation The act of asking for a donation for a charity.

Special Event Any of a number of fundraising events in which the participants are contributing to a charity by virtue of taking part in the event. That is, they are receiving a tangible benefit themselves such as a concert or a dinner. In these cases only the amount of the admission fee that is over and above the value of the event is considered a charitable donation.

Special Names The list of supporters of an organization whose donations are substantially higher than average and who are generally solicited differently than the majority of donors.

Sponsor Someone who is supporting the cost of putting on an event or activity and is receiving substantial exposure in return; usually a corporation.

Sponsorship The act of providing financial support for an event or activity in return for substantial public relations benefit; usually does not qualify for charitable donation status because of the value of the benefit received by the sponsor.

Stamp, Live A term used in direct mail to indicate a "real" stamp as opposed to a metered stamp or a bulk mail indicia. Usually increases response rate.

Stewardship The concept of an obligation by an organization to use donated funds properly. (Also the concept that individuals are responsible for the wise use of all resources. Often extends far beyond fund-raising to include environmental stewardship).

Stop Cards   Instruction on a prospect card or pledge card to stop solicitation for any one of several reasons.

Strategic Plan   Overall long-term direction for a group, including programs as well as fundraising.

Stuffers Volunteers who gather to put together the components of a direct mail package.

Support Piece   An extra part of a mailing in a direct mail package that helps sell the cause or adds additional endorsement by a well-known person.

Supporter   In fundraising terms generally synonymous with a donor, someone who assists a charitable organization with a financial contribution.

Suspect   A potential donor requiring further research to qualify as a prospect. (See Prospect)

Swim-a-thon   A fundraising event in which participants obtain pledges for swimming in the event.

T3010, Form   Revenue Canada's official form that must be submitted annually by all registered charitable organizations on which the executive officers, overall revenue and expenses, and major charitable activities for the year are noted; it is available to the public. There is an accompanying "schedule" which requires more detailed financial and operating information that is not for public information.

Targeting The process of limiting one's fundraising efforts to a carefully selected target market.

Task Force A group of people who work together to accomplish a specific goal, and then disband. Sometimes a better term than "committee" because it indicates the focused, productive, and short-term purpose.

Tax Deduction The term used prior to 1988 in Canada for the tax treatment of donations by individuals to registered charities. The amount of the gift (subject to limitations) was deducted from the donor's income earned. Corporate donations are still tax deductions, while individuals now receive a tax credit.

Tax Credit The term used beginning in the 1988 tax year for the tax treatment of donations by individuals to registered charities in Canada. Now donations (subject to certain limitations) are treated as tax credits which have the effect of reducing the amount of tax payable (rather than reducing one's taxable income).

Taxation Year (See Fiscal Period)

Team A group of volunteers who work together to canvass or otherwise raise funds for a charity.

Team Captain The person charged with leading a team of canvassers or other volunteers in support of a charitable activity.

Teaser copy The term used in direct mail to indicate any information other than the return address that appears on the outside of the mailing envelope. The purpose of the teaser copy is to entice the reader to open the envelope.

Telemarketing The systematic use of telephone calling to donors/prospects to solicit funds. Telemarketing uses either paid canvassers or volunteers.

Tele-thon A fundraising technique in which a variety show is broadcast on television or radio and viewers are asked to phone in pledges in support of the charity putting on the show.

Test List A list of prospect names that is being used to see if the profile of the list will result in an acceptable response rate to a mailing.

Test Mailing A new or different mailing letter or package that is being tested against a control to see if it will out-perform the control.

Testimonial An endorsement or acknowledgement that a charity has been helpful to a client, it could also come from a donor. Used in direct mail or a campaign to lend credibility and/or urgency to the appeal.

Thank-you Letter The letters sent to donors along with their receipt after a donation.

Third Sector A term, more commonly used in the United States, to indicate the not-for-profit sector as distinct from governments (the first sector) and business (the second sector). Also known as the Independent Sector.

Time, Talent and Treasure (TTT) Board members are generally expected to give all three.

Tombola A mystery prize which donors either bid on at an auction or buy raffle tickets to win.

Tracking The process of recording the results of a campaign, especially a direct mail campaign.

Trading The process of exchanging mailing lists between organizations for direct mail purposes (Also known as List Exchanging).

UDs   Undeliverables. Fundraising letters that are returned because of incorrect or out-dated addresses. They must be corrected in the database in order to keep mailing costs down and the list "clean".

United Way A special organization that exists in many communities that exists to undertake a common annual fundraising campaign in order to keep costs down and reduce the number of solicitations that people receive.

Upgrading The process of encouraging donors to increase the size and/or frequency of their contributions.

VLDP Volunteer Leadership Devlopment Program, a training program of United Way/Centraide Canada purchased from the United Way of America and adapted for use in Canada. It is designed to help local volunteer boards improve their leadership skills and to create an opportunity for organizational change.

Volunteer A person who undertakes any of a variety of tasks or duties on behalf of a non-profit organization without financial remuneration.

Volunteer Centre An organization that exists in most larger communities to match volunteers with non-profits which need help.

Volunteer Training A process of educating volunteers in the techniques of fundraising for a particular event or canvass.

Walk-a-thon A fundraising event in which participants obtain pledges for walking in the event.

Webbing The process of actively uncovering the network of people you know that you didn't know you knew, who in turn can be useful in fundraising, on boards, as volunteers or as donors. (See also Hooks & Ladders)

Welcome Letter A more sophisticated version of a Thank-you Letter that focuses on making the donor feel that he or she is becoming part of a special cause or organization because of the donation.

White Mail Donations that come in the donors own envelopes, not a BRE. Sometimes used to refer to all direct mail donations that come in after a campaign cut-off date, whether solicited or not.

Wills Clinic A seminar conducted by or on behalf of a charity in which the mechanisms required for a Last Will and Testament are outlined and the suggestion that the charity could be named as a beneficiary is either stated or implied.

Wish List A list of items that an organization would like to buy for its programs or clients but for which it has no funding. The wish list is presented to prospective donors for them to choose something to buy with their donation.

WHYFU Letter A fundraising letter sent to lapsed donors asking "why have you forsaken us?"

WIIFM   What's In It For Me?   A phrase often asked either directly or implicitly by potential corporate donors when considering a major donation or sponsorship.

Is anything missing?

Did you look for a definition and did not find it?
Please let us know, so we can improve the next
edition of the
Canadian Glossary of Fundraising Terms.

Send us your comments and suggestions:
phone 1-800-387-4020
(in Ottawa (613) 744-7711)
fax (613) 749-9449
or write to
John Bouza & Associates
Suite 202, 16 Beechwood Avenue
Ottawa ON   K1L 8L9

Canadian Glossary of Fundraising Terms

To order additional copies of the Canadian Glossary of Fundraising Terms, *please use this page to place your order by phone or fax, or mail a copy of the form to John Bouza & Associates.*

Quantity discounts are available. Please inquire.

Please rush me _____ copies of the Canadian Glossary of Fundraising Terms at only $9.95 each, plus $2.00 shipping and handling costs per copy. (G.S.T. will be absorbed by John Bouza & Associates on pre-paid orders.) I understand that if I'm not completely satisfied, I can return the *Canadian Glossary of Fundraising Terms* to John Bouza & Associates for a complete refund.

Mailing address   Billing address (only if different from
                                    mailing address)

Name _____   Name _____

Organization _____   Organization _____

Address _____   Address _____

Province _____ Code _____ Province _____ Code _____

Daytime phone _____   Daytime phone _____

❑ Check enclosed payable to John Bouza & Associates

❑ Bill me

John Bouza & Associates
202 - 16 Beechwood Avenue, Ottawa ON   K1L 8L9
fax (613) 749-9449
1-800-387-4020

G.S.T. # R126839679